D0943819

RICHARD RODGERS

NO STRINGS • VOCAL SCORE

A RODGERS AND HAMMERSTEIN COMPANY

NO STRINGS

NO STRINGS • VOCAL SCORE

WILLIAMSON MUSIC®
A RODGERS AND HAMMERSTEIN COMPANY

VOCAL SCORE

NO STRINGS

Music and Lyrics by
RICHARD RODGERS

Book by
SAMUEL TAYLOR

Library Property
Not a Rental Score

Applications for performance of this work, whether legitimate, stock,
amateur, or foreign, should be addressed to:
RODGERS & HAMMERSTEIN THEATRE LIBRARY
229 West 28th Street, 11th Floor; New York, NY 10001
Telephone: (212)564-4000; Facsimile: (212)268-1245

ISBN 0-88188-038-8

WILLIAMSON MUSIC®
A RODGERS AND HAMMERSTEIN COMPANY

EXCLUSIVELY DISTRIBUTED BY

HAL•LEONARD®
CORPORATION

7777 W. BLUEMOUND RD. P.O. BOX 13819 MILWAUKEE, WI 53213

Williamson Music is a registered trademark of the Rodgers Family Partnership and the Estate of Oscar Hammerstein II.

For all works contained herein:
Unauthorized copying, arranging, adapting, recording or public performance is an infringement of copyright.
Infringers are liable under the law.

NO STRINGS

Produced by RICHARD RODGERS in association with SAMUEL TAYLOR
March 15, 1962 at the 54th Street Theatre, New York City

Directed and Choreographed by
JOE LAYTON

Settings and Lighting by DAVID HAYS
Costumes by FRED VOELPEL and DONALD BROOKS
Musical Direction and Dance Arrangements by PETER MATZ
Orchestrations by RALPH BURNS
Associate Choreographer BUDDY SCHWAB

Cast of Characters
(In order of appearance)

BARBARA WOODRUFF	Diahann Carroll
DAVID JORDAN	Richard Kiley
JEANETTE VALMY	Noelle Adam
LUC DELBERT	Alvin Epstein
MOLLIE PLUMMER	Polly Rowles
MIKE ROBINSON	Don Chastain
LOUIS dePOURTAL	Mitchell Gregg
COMFORT O'CONNELL	Bernice Massi
GABRIELLE BERTIN	Ann Hodges
MARCELLO AGNOLOTTI	Paul Cambeilh

DANCERS: Alan Johnson, *principal.* Susanne Cansino, Julie Drake, Jean Eliot, Ginny Gan, Ellen Graff, Kay Hudson, Ann Hodges, Diana Hrubetz, Sandy Leeds, Anna Marie Moylan, Patti Pappathatos, Janet Paxton, Dellas Rennie, Bea Salten, Carol Sherman, Mary Zahn. Gene Gebauer, Scott Hunter, Larry Merritt, Michael Maurer, David Neuman, Wakefield Poole, Calvin von Reinhold.

INSTRUMENTALISTS ON STAGE: *Flute*—Walter Wegner, *Clarinet*—Aaron Sachs, *Oboe*—Ernest Mauro, *Trumpet*—James Sedler, *Trombone*—James Dahl, *Drums*—Ronnie Bedford, *Bassoon*—Walter Dane.

NO STRINGS

Synopsis of Scenes

TIME: The Present

PLACE: Paris

Monte Carlo

Honfleur

Deauville

St. Tropez

Note

The orchestral apparatus of "NO STRINGS" is entirely different from that of the usual Broadway musical play.

There is no orchestra in the pit. The conductor and orchestra are on stage, completely concealed behind the scenery to the right of the audience.

The customary string section is eliminated and the only string instruments remaining are harp, guitar and contrabass (*see Instrumentation below*).

The conductor and orchestra appear on stage only once in full view of the audience after the close of Act. II to play the Exit Music. However, a specified number of musicians *(see below)* do appear and play on stage, either singly or in groups, and are an integral part of the action.

Instrumentation

WOODWIND No. 1: Piccolo/Flute/Alto Flute/Clarinet/Tenor Saxophone

No. 2: Flute/Clarinet/Bass Clarinet/Bassoon/Baritone Saxophone

No. 3: Piccolo/Flute/Oboe/Clarinet/Alto Saxophone

No. 4: Flute/Clarinet/Bass Clarinet/Alto Saxophone

No. 5: Flute/Clarinet/Alto Saxophone

No. 6: Flute/Clarinet/Alto Saxophone

No. 7: Flute/Clarinet/Bass Clarinet/Tenor Saxophone

No. 8: Clarinet/Bass Clarinet/Bassoon/Baritone Saxophone

BRASS: 4 Trumpets, 3 Trombones (3rd Trombone also plays Bass Trombone).

RHYTHM: 2 Percussion, Guitar, Contrabass, Harp, Piano (played by Conductor).

The following instrumentalists also appear on stage: Woodwind Nos. 1-2-3-4, 1st Trumpet, 1st Trombone, 1st Percussion.

Musical Program

ACT I

ACT II

NO STRINGS

No.1 ## Prologue - The Sweetest Sounds

The curtain rises on a darkened stage.

RICHARD RODGERS

Copyright © 1962 by Richard Rodgers
Copyright Renewed
WILLIAMSON MUSIC owner of publication and allied rights throughout the world
International Copyright Secured   All Rights Reserved

M
1503
.R684
N6
1990z

The most en - tranc - ing sight of all Is yet for me to see. And the dear - est love in all the world Is wait - ing some-where for me, Is wait - ing some-where, some - where for

still in - side my head. _____ The

kind - est words I'll ev - er know
The kind - est words _____ I'll ev - er know Are

wait - ing to be said. The

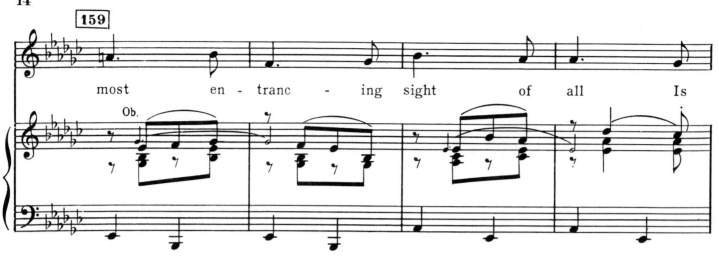

most en - tranc - ing sight of all Is

BARBARA:

Is yet for me to see._____ And the

yet for me to see._____ And the

On stage Fl., Cl.

open Br.

dear - est love in all the world

dear - est love in all the world Is

Ob.

Tpts.

Trbs.

No. 2

Opening Scene Two
(La-La-La)

[Lights up]

Schottische - In 4 *[Flute on platform]*
[Clar. on scaffold]

Piano

No. 3

How Sad

Cue: MOLLIE: I'll give you the short answer. Men.

DAVID: Poor things. What a waste.

gain: _____ How can a wom-an be like a wom-an? What does she see in men? _____

A wom-an's hand is ti-ny; _____ A man has just a paw. _____

Lyrics:
A wom-an's mouth is soft and sweet; A man has just a jaw._____ Be-neath her chin lies heav-en,_____ While un-der his is hair._____ In

Brightly

La - dies, I ask a - gain:

How can a wom - an Be like a wom - an?

What does she see

in men?

No.4

The Sweetest Sounds
(Reprise)

Cue: DAVID: What have you got against Americans?

  BARBARA: Some of my best friends are Americans.

She's real too.

Tutti

Trbs.

simile

+Bsn.

+B.Cl.

28 Ev-'ry-thing a-round us shifts and chan-ges. On-ly we are real. The

Tutti

Glock. [Flute in rt. wing]

32 Moderately-In 2

sweet — est sounds I'll ev - er hear are

On stage Fl.

Trbs.

Hp.

Bs.

still in - side my head.

Fls.

B.Cl.

The kind - est words I'll ev - er know are wait - ing to be said. The most en - tranc - ing sight of all is yet for

Cue: DAVID: I start novels.

[*Solo Ob., crossing from stage right wing to platform.*]

38

1194-187

17 DAVID: You're sure you wouldn't like ... *dialogue continues.*

25

Stop on cue:
BARBARA: Of course you'll have a brandy.

33

L.H.

No. 6   Loads Of Love

Cue: **BARBARA: If it doesn't, I'll take it back and exchange it for another world!**

never have re-ject-ed much. I want my din-ner, Some

con - ver - sa-tion And loads of love-ly love. The

dumb ones go for quan - ti-ty, — The wise ones go for

qual - i - ty. — I've got the an-swer now: It's

not how much, it's how! I do not ask for

bliss, I guess. It all boils down to this, I guess:— I

just want mon-ey, And then some mon-ey, And loads of love-ly

love!

My work ful - fills me; It
nev - er kills me. So far I'm not a
wife, So I or - gan - ize my life so No
one an - noys me, No one en -

Pno., Bs., Gtr.
Tpts.
Saxs.

46

joys me Un - less we're e - qual part - ners in the

54

fun._____ Through the week I

Cl.

Saxs.

Bar.

work and play and give.

Tpts.

p

Trbs.

E - ven on Sun - day I love to live!

f Trbs.

nice po - si - tion, And loads of love - ly love! I _____

do not ask for bliss, I guess. It all boils down to

this, I guess: I just want mon - ey, And

then some mon - ey, And loads, _____

No.7

Change Of Scene
(Loads Of Love)

Cue: BARBARA: Thank you for the walk and the violets.

Moderato *[Bsn. is seated on stage.]*

Slower

On stage Bsn. Solo

mf

[Fl., Ob. and Cl. enter and sit with Bsn.]

No.8 The Man Who Has Everything

Cue: LOUIS: Do you think you will love me?
BARBARA: I hope so.

54

1194 -187

Do Not Mark In Score

hind the wheel of my Fer - ra - ri ____ I can ask for an - y - thing more.

On stage Quartet.....

mf rall.

The man who has ev -'ry - thing has noth - ing ____

+ Off-stage Orch.

p a tempo

R.H.

Till love all his own he can see. _____

cont.

SODERTY
Beethoven in Score

hang so ter - ri - bly straight. _____ My

66

sil - ver is Hall-marked, My glass is Bac - ca - ret; I have

Spoken:

ser - vice for for - ty and eight (peo - ple.) My chi -

74
In Tempo

rop - o - dist vis - its me week - ly. _____ (I

No. 9   Change Of Scene

[Tpt. stands at left-proscenium]

Cue: **BARBARA:** How could you bear to leave it?

    DAVID: For Paris? For Europe? *(exit)*

Be My Host

Cue: **DAVID:** *So very deserving.*

guest you ev - er met.
I'm the
On stage Band
cont.
Saxs.
luck - i - est...
as of yet.
Fl.
3
On stage Tpt., Alto
On stage Fl. 8va
+Tpts.
On stage Band
f
115
Step up and prof - fer me your
On stage Tpt., Trb., Bar.
Fl. 8va, Tpts.
Trb.

all.

Step up and

Step up, I'll prof-fer you my all.

Fl.

Tpts.

Saxs., Trbs.

have my-self a ball.

As re-

We're gon-na have a ball.

As re-

Saxs.

G7

Gm7

C7

Bar.

123

cip - i - ent of the best I am the most.

cip - i - ent of the best I am the most.

Saxs.

On stage Band

Tpts. 8va

+On stage Band

Be my host, be my host, be my

host. _____ Be _____

Cl. 8va

Tutti

Br.

f

_____ my _____

135 GABRIELLE and LUC:

Step up, my

MIKE: Step up, step up, etc.*("barker" spiel)*

(host) friend, and be my host.

+W.W.

mf

On stage Sax., Cl.

Hp.

Step up and of - fer me a toast.

143

I'm the duck - i - est lit - tle guest you ev - er

met. You're the luck - i - est

as of yet.

Dance

La-La-La

attacca

Change Of Scene
(Party Introduction)

No. 13

You Don't Tell Me

Cue: DAVID: Stop backing away.

BARBARA: Stop it! Stop telling me what to do!

tea, And when af - fec - tion starts to take me o - ver,

You don't tell me.

On - ly yes - ter - day

I was green as May.

Now I have to say— I'm wise to cer- tain symp- toms. The young have an op - tion on youth. I'm as young as I ev - er will be. I real - ly un- der - stand the mo - ment of truth._ You don't tell me!

Love Makes The World Go

Warning: **MOLLIE:** And all the world loves a lover.
    [Trombone enters and sits on stage left proscenium.]
Cue: DAVID *throws his glass at one of the overhead lights.*

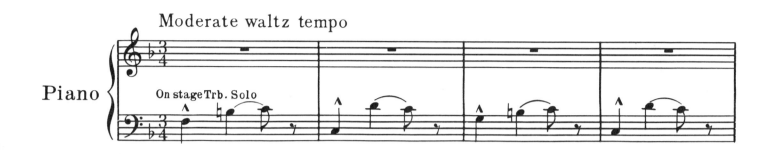

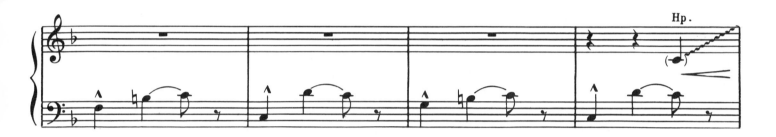

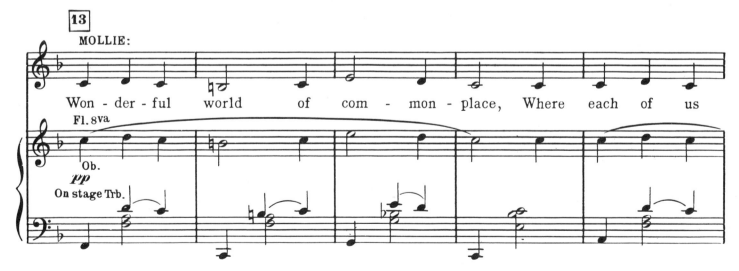

world go square._____ Love makes the world go square.

The race is to the swift, my friend, But

106

1194-187

Cue: *Trombonist starts to exit.*

Vamp - ad lib.

As MOLLIE and COMFORT exit
proceed to bar 236

[Drum solo on stage as scene changes.
Continue ad lib. until DAVID enters.]

Fingers on Tom-Tom

Nobody Told Me

Cue: DAVID and BARBARA embrace

sing to. Night is the on - ly time

When you bad - ly need some - one to Cling to. _____

Cling to me, my dear. Sing to me

all I need made clear.

66 Slowly

BARBARA:

No - bod - y told me Love was like a

whirl - wind. No - bod - y told me

Hp.

+Br.

Cl.

Fl.

(Cl. as before)

Opening Act II
Look No Further

Warning: Curtain rises.
Cue: **BARBARA:** *(off stage)* **DAVID?**

In tempo-Moderately

With love we look at each oth - er, Now we have found what we planned. ___

Cls.

Bell

Hp., B.Cl.

24

Look no fur - ther, Be still. Don't move an inch a - way, stay.

+ Fl.

Cl.

p

Stay with one who loves you. Look no fur - ther, dear.

32

BARBARA:

No more search - ing, That's through. This is the jour - ney's end, friend.

G. Fl.

Cl.

Cl.

right there, Mak - ing me all com - plete, sweet.

Sweet it is to hold you, Look no fur - ther dear.

+Trbs. sust.

BOTH:

Look no fur - ther, dear.

W.W. only +Vlb.

Hp. gliss.

60 BOTH:

Why must you wan - der? Heav - en is - n't far.

col 8va

+Trbs.

(b)

Maine

Cue: BARBARA: Oh, David, how could you bear it?
DAVID: I don't rightly know... but I did.

Make be-lieve all of it's yours. Take a breath, blow it out.

No, it ain't steam. It-'ll be warm-er in-doors. Let the

snow come down be-fore it starts to rain. Un-der the cov-ers

it's co-zy. Far a-way, 'cross the bay Goes an old train:

Read - y for bed. Close your eyes, start to count sheep.

Mu - sic comes float - ing up in - to your head. What's the use try - ing to

sleep? There's a re - cord play - ing in the flat be - low.

Down there a trum - pet blows soft - ly. What a warm place it is af - ter it's dark.

1194-187

Casino Scene - Part I
(The Beach House)

Cue: **DAVID: I don't have to look no higher'n your head for my saviour.**

Cue: DAVID: I've been trying for
years... can't you see? *Dialogue continues*

Casino Scene - Part II (The Ballet)

Casino Scene - Part III

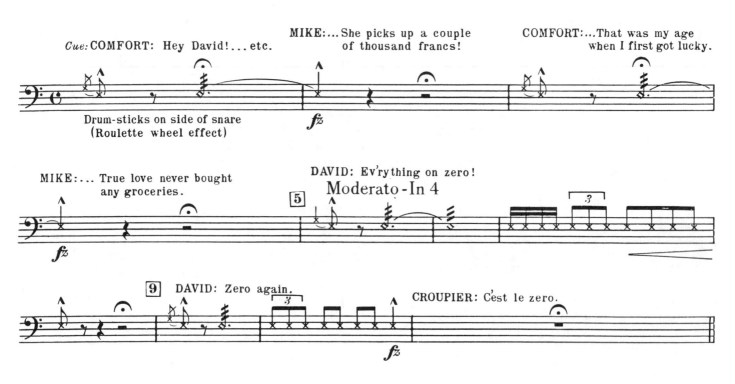

An Orthodox Fool

Cue: LOUIS: And remember the red wine must never be chilled.

ed - u - cat - ed id - i - ot, ___ I'm an or - tho - dox

fool. ___ All I'm not I owe to my - self. ___

Ev' - ry dis - cred - it should go to my - self. ___

I knew my way but I lost it; ___ The game was

Should they have told me Love would come to own me,

Heal-ing and wound-ing me too?_____ No-bod-y

told me, No, not e-ven you. No-bod-y told me, I

knew._____ I'm a

self - ed - u - cat - ed id - i - ot, ___

I'm an or - tho - dox

fool! Fool! Fool! ___

attacca

[*Solo Tpt. is sitting on platform*]

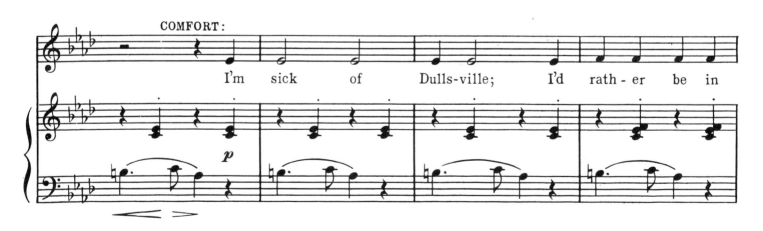

What makes an ea-ger bea-ver try to jump the gun?_____ May-be a bea-ver thinks a bit of rest might cause a mild re-vul-sion,— Or does a feel-ing of com-pul-sion make him run, run,

gun? May - be a bea - ver thinks a

bit of rest might cause a mild re - vul - sion,— or does a feel - ing of com-

pul - sion make him run, run, run? Come, lit - tle bea - ver, I be-

lieve a task a - waits us. Each lit - tle nib - ble brings you

close to where I am.

144
Build like a bea-ver till the thing we're build-ing mates us.

Tpts. 8va

BOTH:
Ea-ger bea-vers al-ways give a dam.

W.W.
Br.

152
Nice lit-tle bea-ver with the skin so soft. Nice lit-tle bea-ver with the

Br.
Dr. etc.

teeth so white, Bea - ver! Bea - ver, we're

right!

Cue. COMFORT: David, I don't want to be alone.
      DAVID: Neither do I.

No. 21a

Change Of Scene
(How Sad)

Piano

No Strings

No.22

Warning: MOLLIE: Girls, I have a present for you. *She exits.*
Cue: *BARBARA and DAVID embrace.*

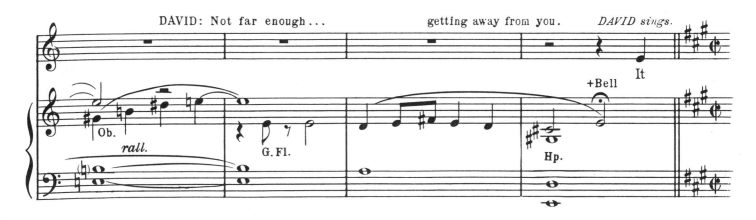

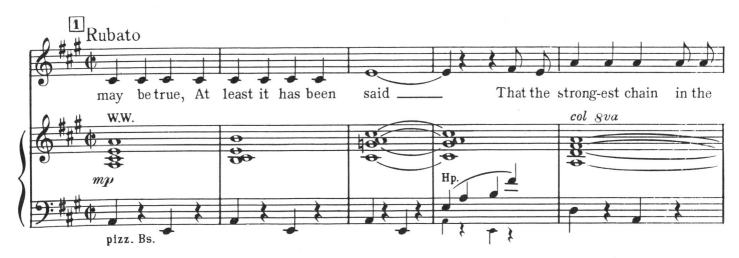

world is a hair from a wom-an's head. But I sus-pect, For us at least, The

strong-est cord of all Is noth-ing, but noth-ing at all. No

strings, no strings, Ex-cept our own de-vo-tion; No oth-er

bonds at all._____ Let the lit-tle folk who need the

No. 23

Maine-Reprise

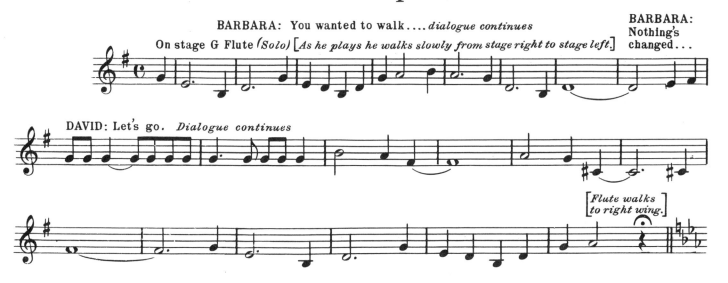

Finale
(The Sweetest Sounds)

No. 25

Curtain Calls
(No Strings)

Stage manager gives cue.

No ties, no ties, Ex-cept our own e-

No. 26   **Exit Music**

Piano

(*Walking Bs. continues*)